For Mike E. :

Life doesn't often give us a new friends to match the old. You are a special exception for me, and I thank you for that — and for your special contributions to the Barons: kindness, enthusiasm, + grace under pressure.

— Mike Daly
9/27/88

THE LIGHTNING TREE SERIES OF CONTEMPORARY POETS

AND OTHER LIGHTNING TREE POETS

SCRIMSHAW: CITIZENS OF BONE

By

MICHAEL D. RILEY

The Lightning Tree—*Jene Lyon, Publisher*
PO Box 1837   Santa Fé, New Mexico 87504   U.S.A.

Michael D. Riley is Assistant Professor of English at Pennsylvania State University, Berks Campus. He and his wife Anne and their two children, Erin Beth and Devin Michael, live in Lancaster.

Library of Congress Catalog Card Number:
87-80649

ISBN: 0-89016-091-0

Printed in the United States of America
FIRST PRINTING
Cover design by John Francis Yeager

THE LIGHTNING TREE—*Jene Lyon, Publisher*
Post Office Box 1837
Santa Fé, New Mexico 87504-1837   U.S.A.

CONTENTS

ACKNOWLEDGMENTS

The author gratefully acknowledges permission from the following publications to reprint poems which first appeared in their pages:

Arizona Quarterly: Macrame
The New Laurel Review: Dancer
Kansas Quarterly: Of a Sparrow, Doris, and John
DLAJ: Emeritus: A Grammar of Assent
Southern Humanities Review: The Crew
Laurel Review: Household
Third Eye: Hands: Abraham Kunstler
Separate Doors: Below the Hill; A Marriage; Old Wood
Minnesota Review: The Man in the Brown Shirt

And God said
Shall these bones live? shall these
Bones live? And that which had been contained
In the bones (which were already dry) said chirping:
Because of the goodness of this Lady
And because of her loveliness, and because
She honors the Virgin in meditation,
We shine with brightness.

—T. S. Eliot, "Ash Wednesday"

MACRAME

We are the weavers
Of intricate knots that connect
Around the holes:

Of great hooting terminals
Switching massive trains of thought;
Of cloverleaves tied into vast bows
To wrap a world of souls;
Of trunklines that slither beneath concrete clothes
To form a net of news;
Above all of synaptic flares,
More numerous than stars,
To surround dead space with clues.

HANDS: ABRAHAM KUNSTLER

Cursed with a body
Stronger than stone,
I lived on, and on,
And do so still, prisoner
Of some dull will and purpose
Buried under skin.
Starvation
Only hollowed every muscle
Into sharper definition.
Doomed at seventeen
To endure in blood and vein
The powerful shell of man,
I became the stranger
Hidden in each pair of hands,
The stranger in my own.
"Iron Cross" they called me,
Salting praise with irony—
I a Jew in recent flesh
Become the spade of Jews beyond redemption,
My iron arms outstretched
Like the heavy wings of earth,
To gather in the dead.

For twenty-seven months
I lugged the guts of other Jews, Gypsies,
Communists, morons with their cow eyes,
The old, lame, sick, at last
Anyone at all,
In wagons, trucks, wheelbarrows,
Many times by hand,

Their soft parts bouncing on the rutted frost,
In spring carving like coulters
Shallow furrows in the mud,
Sliding with odd grace
Until they tumbled, broken, down the sides of pits
And all grace collapsed in heaps.
Legs and arms and backs would snap
Like dead trees in a storm,
And more than once one going down head first
Would break his neck and turn
To fix me with dead eyes.
Women and men tangled
In a parody of love.

So many shades inscribed
The page of flesh:
The bleached chalk of bone,
A gray sky pregnant with snow,
The golden yellow of a finger of wheat.
(Like teeth, one dental student said,
Though only dentists notice.
And only we and lovers, I thought,
While I could think.)
All rolled into my net
Eighteen hours every day—
The flat bellies of starving fish
On a tide that only grew,
As if each body were a cell
And the sea of flesh a cancer.
While I could think,
It seemed a world was dying
But could never quite be done.

By the time the ovens rose
Like churches with small steeples,
The wave had washed away distinction.
Age and disease,
A spirit folded like a letter in a purse
And meant for someone else,
Or signed over like a will
Too soon: these gave way to young women
With bellies still round with hope,
Men heavy with health
As if they still had lives to lead
And somewhere to walk to on strong legs,
Children delicate as orchids
With hands like petals.
I bore them all
As the labor of my hands.

I shoveled till my shovel broke
And dragged until muscles turned to brine,
Turned green and choked
On Zyklon B from going in too soon,
Found lesions bleeding on my hands.
The ovens stripped my eyebrows, arms,
And half my head of hair,
Branded my face with permanent fever
And burned my retina past repair.
Today the world appears to me
A watercolor over gray.
Taste and smell were sanded down the same,
Though nothing but more death
Will unbend and break
The stubborn fingers of my memory.

I pushed in all the other hands I knew
But one pale boy, tiny as a seed,
Not yet fifteen, whose three months' work
Came just before the end
When the Americans arrived
To vomit and to stare,
Who thought perhaps beyond our gates
God left no more for them to see.
They had young hands and faces.
Some no doubt still had souls.

For nearly forty years I kept
With a fine hand all the ledger books
For a small firm on the *Neue Strasse*.
We specialized in art supplies.
Every day I ran my pale blue numbers
As intricate and thin as fingerprints
In perfect order page after columned page
Without error or tedium,
Quite alone.
Retirement merely hollows my time
Deeper into the palms of my hands,
Becoming one more thing to hold
Without complaint.
With no hint of weakness or disease,
This body bears it much the same.
I busy myself with chores about the house.
In my garden, I tend my crops
In even rows, lush and beautiful.
Flowers I must imagine, though.
Somehow their heavy scent gets through,
Like a finger down my throat.

I remember how the spade shook my hands
When I turned my first crop down,
Crimping their bright heads with the shovel tip,
And stopping up their ears with earth.
Now I make my own with silk and twine
From pictures in my books. Sometimes I catch
    in oil
My delicate creations,
Then hang the still life on the wall
Above the flower vase original.
The effect greatly pleases me.

THE MAN WHO WOULD SET
SPRINGS OF WORDS

The man who would set springs of words
For the naked feet of things
Stares hours out of windows
Just to catch the wave precise
Of the squirrel's tail as it breaks
Above a knotted branch of pine,
Or the oriental feather fan
The descending robin touches ground,
The button stare of rats
Bloating by a rusty pool,
The fly who feeds on one blank eye;

Suffers in cheap boots for weeks
To see the sun bolt from its riverbed
Trailing sheets of salmon in waves
Above the waves of salmon-colored seas,
Arriving just upon the verge
On legs shuddering like luffed sails
Becalmed by a chest heaving shallow breaths,
Only to braid more distant muscles taut
And hope to net from simple print
The ache a salmon sunrise draws upon for bait;

Builds the spring like his own house,
One rough board and bent nail at a time,
Sweat beading rosaries inside his shirt;
Yet pleasures in the grip
That swivels forefinger and thumb
Around the cold iron shaft until it warms,

The cedar smell of all good wood,
The shavings in piles curled like petals,
And the give of grain
As purpose pushes home;

Studies craft like a lizard—
Peripherally,
Blood slow as bottom silt
And cold as the current the silt resists,
With skin like a lizard's—thick,
Too knobbed and ugly to be vexed
By time's descendant dream of birds,
Too snug in the milennia
That bristle down his spine;

Knots his heart to a string
And sinks it out of sight
By a mossed rock in the absolute stream,
Just where the sluggish ripples
Slowly close in crystal ice,
Knows where to find it in the spring
When the ice eases with a groan,
Cracks into fingerprints,
Then opens into steam;

Trusts his bleak self
Despite all evidence, all proofs exact
And incontrovertible,
Sits on his stump in faded clothes
And pores over the old news
Of eye and ear,
Cuts with small scissors

Columns of sense
From the scandal sheets and rags
Of his yellow past
As he waits and listens for the clamp
Of sharp teeth and the howl
Not far off
In the heart of the deep woods.

A CHOICE OF LIFE

Perhaps I can live on my aunt's mantel.
I could become her clock,
The Victorian miniature with cherubim
Which drops each minute with a bell
Down a silver and ivory well,
Yet never outruns its golden rim.

I might back into my own photograph,
A study in black and white.
Raffish and straight, biceps like bricks,
A stomach like a trampoline,
I mug for the lens: The Muscleman.
I knew all the body's tricks.
My right foot rests on the running b :d
And the Plymouth shines like a wet ᴐple.
What a car that was! A back seat like a bed.

The Chinese Export vase might do,
Bought for three dollars in 1927.
Squat and regal as the chamberpot
Of kings, yet savaged with a rainbow
Of cranberries and greens
In enameled lines so delicate and fine
They could not be drawn—only wished on.
In its maze of conventional scenes
Lurks perhaps the passion
Passed, in time, to the perfect line,
The subtle scratch of understanding:
The blue wave, the bird's wing,
The golden ring of sand,

The craft of Mandarin remembering.

No. If I am to live on my aunt's mantel,
I must become the porcelain cat,
The dime store cat with cold gray eyes
And plastic flowers in its ears,
Who stalks more motley prey
Among my aunt's old woman noises,
Like the clatter of dry leaves in a cold rain.

THE VIETNAMESE ON EAST ORANGE STREET

Down this old street—
Cold today, its cratered bricks
Pulled in tight against the bleak
January light—
They glide like exotic birds,
Clipping liquid syllables with delicate tongues,
Setting them free
To dip and soar like songs,
Like wings

Beating east
Through elephant leaves of jade
So thick they roof and wall
The sun out of his house,
Where mist rises into steam
Then into torrents by invisible degrees
And the air clings
Like wet clothes all year,
Where the water buffalo plants his mass
One slow hoof at a time,
And a woman with a dancer's body
Bends low among the rice tendrils
In rhythms written in the almanac
Of muscle, blood, and bone,
And on the village wheel of seasons
Grinding down eternity.
Until like portraits
In a sudden green museum,
Paddy and jungle fall still.
The birds tighten on their narrow perch,

Strangling their songs
As they stretch their feathered necks to hear.
Ugly flowers bloom immense
In black and orange rows across the floor;
The wheel unhinges the rutted paths
And crashes through the trees;
The birds wheel and cry
Before they flee down avenues
Instinct almost forgot,
But which circle the world
Like maps in stone
Older than the mind of man

Descending in a Pennsylvania winter, here
On a street whose syllables
Tease my tongue like my own name.
Imagination pulled my hand for years across
      these sills
I thought so thick with history,
Guided my eye past these Georgian rows
So elegant and spare in their geometry,
And groomed to such precise repair:
Past each sandblasted orange brick,
The marble stoops and lintels veined and
      scrubbed
Like a child's face before some holiday dinner,
The cast iron hitching posts—black horses
With a bull's ring incongruous in every nose,
Shutters hanging out of plumb but dyed
With colors deep and rich as blood—
Burgundies and clarets left as stains
Inside the casks of English sailing ships,

The Federal blues like frozen feet
Severed at Valley Forge, the greens of useless
    currency,
The golds of bottomless hope, and greed.

Descended here by me
Huddled in a quilted coat
Inside my ancient Volkswagen,
Quilted, too, across its orange rind
With dents and rusting memories
Of close calls, obstetric dashes
To assorted hospitals, whole gulfs of tears
And jungles of tangled passion on its seats,
Waiting for my mother
And some new report
From the front, some cunning strategy
Her oncologist will devise
To win her war with her own doomed cells,
Amok in riotous independence.

I am home for good
And can wait upon these old stones.
Blown by a gust unlooked for, undeserved,
After years too long by half
Spent waiting for relief
Above Ohio scrub and Georgia clay
And the great black wounds of anthracite
Filling with rusty rain from Binghamton to
    Macadoo,
I have descended to try
With what little voice is left
This black soil, these exquisite streets,

My dying family, my home.

My heater on the fritz
Again, I seek the street.
Beating my arms like wings
Against the frost,
I fight to send new blood
Along my veins.
They pass as I lag behind
To listen, wait, imagine
Separate songs
As we construe our histories
Upon this old street—
Cold today, gusted and gray—
All heading west.
Talons of wind
Clutch our coats and balloon
Them from our backs like ditty bags
Or knapsacks grabbed in the dead of night,
Barely in time.

BELOW THE HILL

With a pop the skin gives way,
The blood gushes boldly as the muscle separates
And the fine bones splinter.
It takes a manly stroke, for the wood too is hard,
The hammer heavy and the nail outsized.
The soldiers smirk and drink.
Their dice wink like eyes upon a purple cloak,
Snake eyes.
A few women bow bewildered heads to earth.
The crowd lingers a while, then strays
As the blood congeals and the end drags on
Uncomfortably, predictable and crude,
With low moans and fainting:
One thin man, grimy and pale,
Hung out on the line of his own will
While the soldiers get stewed.

Below the hill, men with dusty feet lean toward the gates
And home, weary with another day
Spent trading dates for olive oil, olive oil for dates,
Or scratching hard ground for hireling pay;
Women skim sighing kettles, bending low
With duty above their old domestic debts
While the children play draughts and turn-peg in shadows
That begin to cool as the day slows and hesitates.
The news reaches down, of course, but does not unsettle
A tired man's dinner: another debt Rome owes.
He knew Barabbas, too, had hopes that bled,
A past and promises that now ran red
Upon the clay and sank into the ground.

Beside the cooling hearth, he tore his black bread
And ate without a sound.

JUDAS

"Lawyer," they joked, "Scrollmaker."
As if to read and think betrayed instead of bound
Together, as if to be the hound
Of meaning and worry the brush for clues
Along the crooked scent of truth
Were not the purple and the crown of man.
Such was their simplicity,
They could never see relation, choice, complexity.
At best they petted me with one free hand
While they chatted past me round the fire,
Like a dog they kept for sport
But never sent to field
Because they never knew the game.
I smiled and watched the time
Without resentment. They would never see.
And I was too thrilled
By the chase and chance of history.

He lived among my dreams deeper than desire,
Mingled like breath about my being,
Folded my sinew into praying hands
And swelled my heart with my doom of blood.
Each look, each word
Became the bones that held me up.
As on those bitter nights when the mist stood
In walls around our meager fire
And our hearts ached like our feet
With stones of ignorance and doubt,
He would talk us into palaces
And beds of down until, drunk with promises

And trust, we slept like children
On dead ground.

Once, on the salt sea
In our rough boat, he stood
Like a picture in the prow
And wove the sea and sky together
With words. His hair shivered
As if the fingers of a girl
Had just released it strand by strand,
And his cloak fell in sculptor's folds
Below his shoulders.
When he cupped the wind
Between his hands,
The slotted sea rose up, curled
In whiter ringlets and lifted all of us,
Then froze the world one timeless breath—
Before it so slapped and shook the hull
We pitched from our seats like dolls.
That moment, one at balance on the scales of death,
I like an artist felt forever.

How could I fail to fight against
What I alone could see?
The wreck of all upon these local rocks,
His death hanging in his eyes
Like curtains in a window,
Each of us a corpse stiff and twisting in a tree,
With so much left to do,
He in his prime and all so well begun.
Could I let such promise slip into the trough

Of politics, become a gristled bone
For the starving dogs of faction?
Be ground into mush
By the stone wheel of a worn-out law?
Or wash into sewers through the dull greed of Rome?
Only to find *my* promises
Swept off the temple floor next day
Like so much tainted straw.
That money burned my palm like thirty glowing coals
And stunk in my nostrils
Like the dung of thirty mules.
(I flung it to earth among olive trees.)
I only wanted more.
More time to burn the rust
From our benighted country, and ourselves,
Guarantee the future with a plan,
Declare our proofs, research and organize.
More time to understand.

Love alone hated me.
He left me only life:
A bag with a drawstring like a noose
Dropped down a midnight well
Or scattered like seed under olive trees
When the wind kicked the crowd's angry voice
Like a child's ball to and fro
And bent their torchlights down,
One voice rolling from Jerusalem
To pound my head in waves of blood.
Love in that purple grove felt like hate,
Heavy as the bag of flesh I could not pinch off

Soon enough with hemp, to strangle thoughts
That tasted once like fresh mint-silver drops
But now melted on my swelling tongue
Like wafers of decaying meat.

DANCER

The rain of early spring rattles the unraked leaves
Littering my yard until they leap with a sound like
    castanets
Heard far off and hollow.
The great evergreen rooted by my window
Lifts, lets fall, entwines its limbs
In the Oriental gusting winds.
Down the tree's thick heart a squirrel sweeps
    his contradance,
Stares in, spins with infinite grace, disappears.
The rain drums louder on the metal roof,
Like fire-hardened sticks on hollow logs
In prelude to some ritual violence,
Put to proof in a blur of spinning feet and sound
Until the rain floods my labyrinth of spouts
And falls in spears upon the ground.
My hands hang slack between my knees.
I sit and wait, my chair flat against the wall.

Stiff in the grip of her partner pain,
My mother's arms and legs move strange and slow.
His muscular forearm bows her chest
And steals the breath we thought to save,
Designing to dance her out of time
In one dying fall from grace.
Breath rattles in her chest
As she lies in bed and demands the spring.
It's in the bone, the doctor says.

She who spun years ago

On every East Coast polished floor
From New York to Baltimore
Until dawn broke into roses
All the dusty dancehall windows
And the band packed up, too tired to go on.
Now other drugs spin through her limbs,
Glaze her blue eyes, lead her will
With their violent tenderness,
And contract the rings of her heart.
Yet cortisone rounds her face
Until she seems to me a youthful Balinese,
Needing only finger-tambourines,
A skirt of billowing red and gold,
Gold anklets, bracelets, necklaces
Drumming like a thousand tiny bells
To break her beauty on this vinyl corridor
And shock with noise and color
This dance floor filled with gliding ghosts.
But only our eyes keep time.
I sit and wait, my chair against the wall.
Her green quilted robe
Shapes her like a shell
And holds her still.

I rise and bend down.
We move together among dead leaves
Stirred by warm rain in rhythms not our own.
But we will be the season's thieves,
Stealing melodies beyond the bone
Whose rhythms lead us to embrace,
Face one another, dance.

A GENERALIZATION OF FOWLS

Not a charm of finches
Merely,
Nor always a newborn peep of chicks.

Not forever
The spring of teal
Rising like sap through old trees
Toward a sky perfectly blue—
Only to give way themselves
To an exaltation of larks.

The congregation of rooks convenes
To bless the dictates
Of the parliament of owls.
A muster of peacocks
Marks the fall
With bold parades
Across the stubble fields.

For a while
A wave of warblers
Crests in song
Above a paddling raft of ordinary
    ducks
Weaving toward white water and
    the rocks
Beneath a watch of nightingales
Snug at home
In their house of trees.

Then what stirs
(Always stirs)
The murmuration of starlings?

A murder of crows
Declining black wings
Toward snow
Above a whiteness of swans.

OF A SPARROW, DORIS, AND JOHN

With one more wild request for love, John
Hunched on his knees against the garden wall.
He missed the sparrow's fall,
Rooted as he was upon the ground.

The bird was unlovely anyway, plain, no great shakes
At singing, either, if the truth be known.
Dun among green leaves and rainbow petal flakes
He seemed a twig, a wind-up bird of brown.

The blue day, the buzz of life all around
Of course denied it all: the soft plummet like a
        hollow stone,
His stiff-legged salute once he hit the ground,
The way he redefined the rest, upside down.

John pressed against his passion in the dust,
Cajoled his deities large and small,
But two thighs beneath a desk in the office of lust
Scissored his devotions and let their fragments fall.

Feathers of skin teased him by the hour,
Small stabbing eyes of black, her spindly grace
On tall stiletto heels, her sharp symmetric features.
        Her power
Of body wrung his neck and dropped him in his
        place.

HUMBERT HUMBERT'S SONG

Upon these perfect pins stands all
That for a while
I love.

My will tightens
Along each crease
Of her pink shorts;
Her strawberry gum bubbles and pops
On the old stove of my heart.
Each "yeah" and "y'know" sweetly raps
Upon my neural telegraph
Uncluttered sonnets past the reach of art.
Her thighs compress, diverge,
Then merge into her laugh,
A belly laugh.
I love each tune to which her pink toes tap.
Their insipid lyrics light up my life.
In the cradle of her lap,
I rock the past to pieces with delight.
Venus on the half shell,
She rises from my seas at dawn
Erect in all her power
Of buttock, thigh, and fatted calf.

Between her soft covers
I am rolled in the heroic mold.
Her Delft blue eyes tilt me toward
The windmills of the world
As I grasp her yellow mane of hair
And ride beyond redemption.

I am stout Balboa
Straddling twin peaks in Darien,
Come to kiss his dream
Still moist upon the edge of ocean.
Seduced by such sweet science,
I am tireless in my field research:
Triangulating moles,
Graphing dew points of pores
In steep parabolas,
Testing with endless windings
The texture of each hair
Between my caliper fingers;
Testing between micrometer lips
The smallest fact of flesh.
I am willing to be crucified
With bright red nails.

My treatise on Tocharian,
My book on Linear B
Curl in corners like dead skin.
Yesterday a crosswind blew
Fifty folds of manuscript
Right out one open window.
I watched them settle like fat flakes
        of snow
On the honking traffic far below.

All the idolators of mind
Will never find
The secret secret tucked within
A plowed field of perfect skin,
Hidden between a pair of lips

Pouting like sliced plums,
Never find in footnotes
Such perfect feet
Or hold in all their paper clips
Pages like these thighs
Scrimshawed with microscopic runes
No sublimation can surprise.
I never answer
When they ring me on the phone.
I am much too busy standing here
In robe and slippers
By my kitchen stove,
Whistling Telemann's old tunes
As I brew her cup of tea.

A MARRIAGE

We lie in bed and stare
As the ceiling closes down.
I feel your snarled hair and flannel gown
In the intervening air.
You feel my receding hair
And dreams. Habit hears
The shrill contention
Down the hall. I lie alone
As your image empties our mirror.
You have flown
To calm the future once again. The spare
Imprint of your body stirs
The hollows of desire
And the gray face of dead plans.

You in yellow silk
Like a second skin
Bent like a bow by passion,
Or tatting centaurs and unicorns
Before a satisfied fire.
I before a line of books
Unable to knit your looks
Of love in words, but eager to essay
      again
As the children sleep off their innocence
In beds of bold dreams,
Then wake with us at dawn
To long hours of excellence.
Or we preside
Over simpler dreams

At a country oilcloth board.
A flutter of grandchildren
Peck your skirts or fly
Through the ancient house we restored
To the last handmade nail
And filled with the clutter of shared
    effort,
The portage of years required
To take the measure of mature emotion
And learn to savor in love a modest
    portion,
Robust and sweet as homemade wine.
On a porch anchored in vines,
Loud with honeysuckle scent
And the swell of crickets,
Our lips would touch their settled smiles
And fingers thread lightly
Their circle of old signs.

Love in its flesh we hardly know.
Something to dull the point,
Slow the skewer of our mortgaged box
By debts too great to pay,
Or cover with snow, like the garbage in
    the yard,
Something to throw like sulfa
On the mortal wound we carry in our
    laps,
A sharing beyond all platitude
And hope.
We search the faces of our dreams
Like those in the convenience store

For one with skill
To sell us rope enough.
But we turn white in one embrace
Beyond the soothe of fingertips,
Others and our own.
We are citizens of bone.
The old toy of divorce
We save fondly
As a childhood souvenir.
Lawyers in horn-rims
Clacking like dry reeds,
Neurotic children whining through
A crowd of stuffed animals and promises,
Saturday matinees
And Sunday visits to the Zoo:
Such knots would hang us both
At whatever age or distance.
We have been cast like dice
Past single resolution.
We gambled just that much
Too much.
As you pad across this mirror
In your pink slippers and private agony,
I will never see you there
Without seeing me.

HOUSEHOLD

He waits upon small things:
Servant of ashtrays, gleaner of lint
From carpets of intermediate cost.
Doorman for the suburban soul,
He empties his life without stint
Into tupperware containers, trashbags, golden rings.

    Outside, the profligate trees strew
    Themselves; his rake snares too few.

Easy chairs remember him long after he is gone.
Springs and foam rubber frame
His good intentions, with no hint of blame:
They exhale his presence like a dry bone the skin.

    The countless printed leaves blow by,
    Dead or dying at this distance from the tree.

Dry cereal rattles in a cold bowl,
Beer whitens and slides down the sides of the glass.
He has beds to make, clothes to unsoil,
Children's questions to avoid, a pain like gas
Upon his chest: He is not heart-whole.

    The mower sputters till it roars,
    Scattering leaves like desperate semaphores.

His wind-up clock ticks true, yet truer time
He marks by sandwiches, the mail, TV,
The remorseless film of domestic grime

That returns to every corner: his own memento mori.
His vacuum cleaner runs on brine.

    Mulch marks the leaves' dry retreat
    In neat rows, like these suburban streets.

An adventure film cuts across his midday screen,
Bristling with courage and duty:
The sheik's smile salutes the hot sun
Like the scimitar he holds wih his hard arm;
Women bend before him their veiled mystery,
And the heads of his enemies grin in the dust.

    He folds up the news and puts more water on
        to boil.
    A maple leaf slides off the window sill.

A VERSE FOR THE LAST
CHRISTMAS CARD

I bring with me
Only these few
Alive in the ion cloud
For one more day,
Maybe two.
We could find
No one else
And nothing more to do.

We have not one scrub bush,
Certainly no tree
To decorate
Or hold us up with nails,
Neither nails nor hammer
For that matter,
Nor strength to push
Them if we had.
Our only stars
In all this fog
Are lanced in red
By rubble on our feet.

For snow
We have this ash
We wear like skin.
It hangs in socks
Upon the stumps
Of trees and posts and feet.
As it melts

We bloom with sores
As round and hard as holly
    berries.

Our incense spirals up
From rocks
Crumbling, like us,
Into powder from within.
Since we cannot stand,
We kneel
Until we fall
Upon our sides,
Like a fetus
Dropped from a dry womb
Onto filthy straw.
The kings of earth
Have passed by here
Already.

Come quickly.
Soon we must be found
Hung upon the high hills,
Our hands and feet entwined
In wreaths of bone.

THE CREW

Our withered arms strained as the oarlocks
    groaned.
Sea-foam riffled our gray heads
Until our beards dripped with sea wrack
Around our tightening smiles:
The rictus of our fate.

The bottom boomed against the waves
Like bone against slate.
The sail luffed and yawned
Until its ragged edges seemed
The fraying beard of one more mariner.
We slid upon the seats like fish
And rowed just to hold to something harder than
    ourselves.
He said again:
Let your muscles ripple up those tattered sleeves
And fingers study every grain of oar!

Most mad, indeed;
Yet he saw in us the iron arms and eyes
Of old, and made us remember:
What our wives threw off soon after
We lay with them as girls
Among the wild goats and sharp gray rocks
Under that uncanny light:
What our children never knew

He knew of course
Our stooped wives and narrow pensions

Had grown as stale in their turn
As his baffled ambition.
The grandchildren in their smocks and lace
Were dear, to be sure;
But indulgence soon had run its course.
We had pulled the world in our wake
Once. The world!
Yet now a glazed mirror
Sought to forge upon history a spectre
Grizzled and lame, gray and harmless as a dove;
We who had thought death himself love
Once, so taut had life been strained
Against the spar.

So we went.
Gladly. More mad by far than he,
Buoyed as he was by destiny.
Bewildered tears and rage
Broiled around the pier.
Angry women, embarrassed sons,
Daughters with stern faces dandling young ones
Milled about distractedly.
But we knew. More than ever now
As the wind spun and swelled the sails
Above our gray faces
And the rope rubbed our hands raw
Once more.

AN IMAGE FOR JANE AUSTEN

The old storm raged long:
It sent spray two streets back from the ramparts
Of Portsmouth, where the ships spun in a drunken reel,
Bobbing like corks; casks of claret and Madeira
Split and disgorged; spilled China tea
Lent fragrance to the rolling holds.
The wind screamed against Lyme's pale cliffs,
Splintering the bathing machines
And sending their boards to sea.
Throughout our island estate trees bent like wheat
And broke, and the deer huddled in dread.

Inside we kept alive:
Thunder behind the damask added counterpoint
To the regulated contra dance from the pianoforte.
Conversation crackled like the fire
And filled the room with conscious warmth.
(Yet that shivering windowpane.
Somewhere lives a liar:
Everywhere.)
Crystal sparkled, the candles and the ladies glowed,
The mood was crisp: silk rustled in our veins.
The mantel shone. A kinsman's countenance
In ivory shifted in the glimmer of the fire
From smile to frown and back again.
The talk went on, and filled the air.

The group was small, intimate by desire.
Yet great mirrors on the walls multiplied the light
And made us seem a crowd.

The assembled harmonies of the contra dance arose
And soon assembled us: rhythm cast us all together,
Feet, hands, and eyes until our narrow room began to move
As each heart does when, for once, it feels and knows
Together, stealing moments of illumination, and of love,
Emerging with the valid minimum we do:
Come together in a hollow house when the winds blow
Wildly through the garden roses, and the hedgerows
Cling together; when the petals and leaves
Strew themselves insanely all along the formal paths,
And the great oak in the center splits, yet stands.

LAZARUS

Now my life dances to disappear
Upon my tongue and fingertips,
Past the curtains of my nose and ears
And the gauze before my eyes.
My mind waits on a wooden bench apart.

The leading-up remains with me
In bold strokes, the gravure of skin and bone:
My body like a fired iron
Pressing the pallet with a weight
Like all flesh gathered in one man of stone,
My fever searing the linen,
Sweating into steam
(So at least sensation made it seem).
To call you with one finger curled
No tighter than your longest ring of hair
Spilled acid oceans in my eyes
And stunned me into rigid sleep—
A sleep whose thunderhead of dreams
Told instinct to expect the storm.
Then one afternoon the sun fell into my head,
     my heart,
Melting every bone with pain.
And then. . . I cannot say.
I saw two ragged lines below your eyes
And felt them channel mine like scars.
I can see them even now.
Those he failed to take away.

Sometimes I seem to feel or see or hear

The round weighted coins upon my eyes, the
    muffled bells
Of voices and clumsy shuffle of feet,
One grasping cry thrust up like a spear,
The cool moist of oil sliding perfume on
The scraping scent of laundered cloth,
The ride uneven over lurching ground
Into dead air smothering with cold,
A silence come alive once the grating roar of
    stone
Sealed itself, and died.
Then a growing lemon slice of sky,
The weight of coins falling
Past my ears, their ring upon the floor,
Groans of a boulder moving
And the dribble of smaller stones among the
    dust,
The gauze brightening before my eyes,
The first breath shaking my chest like a fist
Until it falls like the sun into my heart
And softens my bones with life.
I cannot be sure.
What I remember seems a kiss,
Two bodies forgotten into one.

Forgotten in his eyes,
I thought, as he stood motionless as any stone
Within the surging crowd, his eyes
On me at war with our necessary lies.
My faltering steps stuttered toward you both,
My mind reeling to its knees
Like the swooning crowd beating their breasts

And souls in ecstasies of fear or joy (I could
    not tell)
Until in loving dread you led me home
To bury me deep within your warm tomb of
    arms.

Here in this olive shade, whittling alone
The green wood of my time—
My knife and fingers stuck with sap,
Or by the brown river lost
At school among the silver arcs of fish,
Lingering above my bowl of lamb,
Or in the wicker frail your arms can weave
To hold me fast as we renew
Our youth beneath a once-familiar moon,
I start and tremble on the edge
Of storms which never come.
I find only instants blown away
Past blue puzzle pieces cut from the sky by olive
    leaves,
Or lingering like memories
In water, a fish's tail before my eye
After the sinuous fish is gone,
Or like the tang of earth ripening for years
In flocks into the meat melting on my tongue,
Or in your lips turned into a taste
Between citrus and the heavy musk of dates.
Your skin into a combed field of grain
Where my fingers run, like boys, forever.

This body I wear like old clothes
You feel cold at times. I see in your eyes

50

The dead man in your arms.
Yet we have sealed the mystery
With kisses
And learned to haunt our fingertips
Like ghosts.

OVERHEARD ON THE PATIO:
ONE SUBURBAN MEMORY

I have put on the armor of my years:
A Lay-Z-Boy recliner, philosophy,
A certified Serta perfect sleeper, peers
Who look on me indifferently,
Wife house dog children, a suburban memory
That takes me to the decaying core
At my appointed times, then straggles free.

For I am not far from downtown, by car.

It took years to come this far; the price was high,
Inflated during youth. Things are dear
These days. Take the view from my library.
The way the book-lined window leads the eye
To settle on green hills that seem near;
Imagine the cost that keeps that scene together.

Yet I am not far from downtown, by car.

Or take my family. Love is dearer yet
These days. Just to meet our bare necessities
Strains resources till we groan, grow silent,
Only to begin again. We yearn to fall apart.
The children grow impatient, improvident;
My wife grows weary wearing out her heart.
To hold this house together takes its toll.

None of us is far from downtown, by car.

Someone's murdered every day, it seems.
I admit it, I'm afraid. I lock my store of dreams
Each night, and make the windows fast.
The thieves of love and life have the last
Word; I have only my domestic schemes.
So I have retreated, but not too far.

Each day I go downtown, by car.

THE MAN IN THE BROWN SHIRT

The man in the brown shirt appears
In the alley at the end of our yard,
Peers through the rosebush screed
Odd hours of the week
Long minutes at a time.
The tip of his cigarette
Glows like a tiny fuse
Among the blood red evening roses.
Sometimes he leans against the metal fence
Until it groans like rusty bedsprings.
He stares in at us
With invisible eyes
(We see them with our skin),
Then unhurriedly retreats
Just ahead of the police.
The dog bloodied his snout
Against the chain links
Or choked against his leash,
Until he discovered the poisoned meat.

We crease the curtain edges
With tentative fingers.
Mother in the kitchen
Fumbles her dishes, then turns out the light
And twists her wedding ring
Until she rubs her finger raw.
The nights father waited
Underneath the roses, the man never came
    at all.
For the rest, not all of father's rage

And all his courage
Could send youth into his legs
Or make our backyard small.
All he found among the roses
Was the rough scent of spent tobacco.
Now he seldom tries at all.
The price of a pistol shot
He still finds too high.

My sister prowls the house
As if our walls were bars,
Drums her bitten fingernails
Upon the tables, doors, her knees,
And forgets to wash her flowing hair,
She frets her beauty
Into smaller pieces every day,
While her eyes run away.
Her young lover blustered
For a while, performed
Surveillance from his new car
Briskly for a week or two.
Now he never even phones.

Sometimes late at night
The brown shirt with its fuse
Snakes by out front
Inside a battered pickup truck,
Its fenders rippling in the streetlight
Like the skin of rotten fruit.
Once I spot him from my bedroom window,
I stare for hours from our darkened house.
He never comes again.

But the grimace of his grille
Settles in my dreams
Like the white lips of a corpse.

We no longer chase him with words.
He ran our syntax dry.
Yet in the text
Of one another's eyes,
We always see him standing there.
He heads our silent table;
He joins us in bed,
At work and school.
His dense presence
Defiles us in a thousand ways
Each day, murders
Our family cell by cell.
We cannot help but dwell
On what each of the others knows
Too horrible to tell,
Cannot help but hear
Each ugly syllable
Of every ugly word
The man in the brown shirt
Never says.

THIS QUITE SPECIFIC SUNLIGHT

This quite specific sunlight
Warms my bare arms almost to the bone
As it takes yellow bites from the green wreath
Of particular leaves
Tangled above my head
Each time one exact slant of breeze
Stirs them out of shade.
Ropes of honeysuckle scent
Knot me fast
As my hands heft my weight
To balance in nests of damp grass.
I am rooted like this oak.
Yet still some aftertaste of thought
Vexes my palate, troubles my throat
And plays against my tongue
Like an old song,
Even here at the very end
Of my ordinary yard.

The molecules kiss, cling, uncouple,
Change partners to pursue
The promise locked away
In matter's dark, promiscuous heart.
Their orphans spin their simple plans alone.
In May rings the electrons dance,
Hems of dresses in their hands
And hair streaming free.
The protons balk with temporary pride,
Hitch their trousers and plant their feet,
But soon fall in behind the lifting skirts,

Lock hands and hurtle on.
Upon his porch the stolid neutron sulks,
Old age a taste already on his lips.
Then he reaches for his pen.

The enzymes puzzle out their strands
Of love in hair upon a pillow
Or in the gold and silver streaks gathered
In the wheel of one blue eye
Before the eyelid melts them down
In sleep to run through veins of a deeper mine
And bury chemistry within the soil of dreams:
Where souls on stems
Dance gracefully a day,
Presenting with soft hands
A perfect rose.

From its ordinary yard
The eye plucks itself a piece,
Some green particle
Fit for simple sowing,
As the ear breaks into lessons
The heaving of wind against the trees
Or syllables from soft lips nearby,
As fingers fold the rough fuzz peach
Carried from the house
Or the wet skin of this single blade of grass
Into words just out of reach
Of tongue and taste and touch.

ASSIGNATION

When the spell rolls over
Like a tired lover
And sags into simple sleep;
When the mood shifts
And the moon slips by the prism
On the bureau,
Erasing its rainbow from the wall
And leaving a shell
In heavy glass;
When the insight withdraws
Small step by step
Down the old stairs from what it loves
And takes the snowy road toward home;
When the moment lifts up like mist,
Reimposing on the eyes
Furrows like fists
In the hard ground,
I resist.
And by resisting feel
The eggshell ice
Compact and splinter underneath my heel
And heavy boots,
And feel farther down
Green roots
Just pretending to be brown.

EMERITUS: A GRAMMAR OF ASSENT

One of the "eminent dinosaurs" am I, John?
Well, leaving Dean Mallard's politesse behind
(His either-ended smile), I've half an "aye"
To give the epithet. Lately the woods
Seem thicker, and my bulk extends beyond my breath;
A brontosaurial heaviness weighs
Down my thoughts, indeed. The museum *may* be next.
Scut! Let him do his worst. I'm half past caring
And tired to the very bone. The dregs of my
Ambition could be stored in the bottom
Of his coffee cup. And his Young Turks bore
And anger me by turns with their febrile
Self-concern, their politics, that most odd
Pomposity of youth. Lord let them rise
And be a name: the chiefest feather
On Stephen Duck, John Clare the Water Poet's
Raft and oar, all Grub Street's kennel broom!

Lord save us, John! Either I deserve the toe
Of your glossy English boot, or else my dotage
Opens up a new career: curmudgeon.
And why not? God knows they need a scourge.
I could whittle a stout shillelagh,
Don my academic gown and mortarboard
And roam the halls to rail against the times
And pillory the bureaucrats, the shallow
Snobs, the blank pragmatic young
With their statistical souls—striking at night
(My gown aloft) to torch these dungheaps
Of computer cards, jargon, illiterate reports;

Deans, Bursars, and Vice-Presidents would lie
In clumps, their eyes locked in their weasel stares
Forever, a neat red "F" between them.
Quietus causa? A heart thrust with a cheap Bic pen.
(Nothing over nineteen cents; I'll need a lot.)
The Luddite of Literature rides again!

Too late, John, much too late. How does that mucker
Mallard put it? "Retrenchment requires. . .
Accountability (of course: the ledger sheet). . .
Years of distinguished service. . .perhaps a rest
Well-earned. . .Enrollment, at the best,
For medieval studies, after all. . . ."
The hypocrite: His ducats and my daughter.

Yet it was not always so, and more and more
I find myself needing to remember.
Do you recall the Greek Revival tower?
(God, no! Not that penile shaft on the square,
The Trustees' Freudian whimsy.)
No, this one stood by the old Lyceum
In a small grove with benches—gone years ago.
It had the most resonant carillon,
Pealing matins, vespers; so they seemed, at least,
To me, standing by this window listening
While the sun sat in that gnarled tree—gone now,
Too, I see. Strange! only to notice now.
Sprinkled students were trysting or reading.
Unlike those hurrying ones below.
Those notes seemed somehow to ring out over years,
Along the rough coast of an ancient sea.
I almost felt the ceinture round my waist,

The weight of my woolen cloak, wet from the sea
    wrack;
Heard the scrape of vellum; smelled the incense
    smoke.
At dusk I stood watch for Columba's sail
Upon the stormy Irish sea—so drunk
With hope and the music of vocation:
        The rasp of keys in many locks,
        The chain-weight heaving from the hasp
           to the ringing floor,
        The sweet heft of vast, priceless books
           to men bent upon the timeless chore
Of love: illumination.

    Sunlight falls from the latticed heights
    Of narrow casements
       into pools of liquid gold,
    Sets fire to crimson vials, more red
       than the memories of lips,
    Burnishing plates of molten emeralds
       with an ecstasy of tints.

    Across the stiff vellum
    Meticulous brushes move like needles
    With infinite deliberation,
    Scoring mere skin with beauty,
       and forcing from slow time
    A living memory:
    A moment when love and faith
    Held poor wisdom close.

Forgive an old man his ration of romance,

But I've begun to know the dancer from the dance;
And images of late too real
For memory trouble my sight, my soul.
Almost all dead now, John, but you, and each
Glimpse over years more uncertain or false
Than the one before: even dear Mary's face
Forced now to live merely among my nerves and
        bones.
Enough. Or too much. Although I have not
Miles anymore to go before I sleep,
I do have a class to try to reach,
If I can.

OLD WOOD

I would choose, he said, for my final afternoon
A quiet pub slowly filling up with smoke
Aromatic as the burning leaves
Of ancient Eastern trees;
A pub of old mahogany,
Dark and heavy as the weight of another time,
Rubbed to a glow by endless backs and knees,
By slow stories and civility;
A pub with sawdust on the floor
And the sweet smell of spilled beer,
Where an old man gnarled like hickory
Would turn to me above his pipe
And say:

"I have seen my dreams
Gather like mist in the tangled boughs of trees
Then burn off with the sun of each new day;
At dusk I wrote down their forms and themes
As the clouds curled in again."